Designerly ways of knowing: a working inventory of things a designer should know

Danah Abdulla

T0043970

Introduction

On 26 March 2020, architect, urban designer, activist, and critic Michael Sorkin died at the age of 71 after contracting COVID-19. A prolific writer, Sorkin was best known for his irascible critiques and joyful humour, as is apparent in "Two Hundred and Fifty Things an Architect Should Know," an essay-list which recently became a posthumous book. While trapped in my flat during the first UK lockdown, I became inspired by Sorkin and I began compiling my own list, asking myself: *can the designer think*? Design must be theory informed and intellectually rigorous, and designers should consider how the rigour of research is implemented in practice and reflected on. Unfortunately, design thinking has created divisions between the intellectual designer and the practitioner. Either you are too theory driven (or perceived as much) or simply a practitioner.

Despite the currency of design thinking from the early 2000s to today, where design has become the secret weapon of businesses and governments, the designed world looks and feels almost exactly the same. Design thinking does not magically rid the world of bias, it is now masking it under the guise of innovation. Design thinking has crippled designers to generic tools and methods. If you take away the post-it notes, the A3 papers and the markers, can the designer *think*?

In posing these questions, I compile a list based on a search for knowledge and a designer's commitment to making the world a better place. I recall Antonio Gramsci's advice on how to think and know critically:

> The starting-point of critical elaboration is the consciousness of what one really is, and is "knowing thyself" as a product of the historical process to date which has deposited in you an infinity of traces, without leaving an inventory. The first thing to do is to make such an inventory[1].

I take Sorkin's list and I compile one for designers, keeping some lessons he mentioned that are relevant to designers and adjusting them when necessary. The list is generic – it applies to all designers no matter their specialisation, as every designer also needs to be a generalist. The list is a work in progress, ending at **240** items. It is, as any piece of design, an iterative work.

The list is not in any particular order and there are items that people might agree or disagree with. This list is not to be seen as a definitive "how to" guide, but to spark conversations, to prompt critical thinking and to help designers reconfigure their discipline. Therefore, there is no 'correct' way of using it. First performed as a text during the Back to the Future conference organised by Loughborough University in July 2021, as a publication, the text invites readers to contribute their own items or rewrite existing ones by leaving space on the pages. My intention is to constantly iterate this list, and I invite readers to share their items by using the hashtag *#240designerlythings*.

1. Hoare, Q. and Nowell Smith, G. eds., 1999. *Selections from the Prison Notebooks of Antonio Gramsci*. London: ElecBook.

240 things
a designer
should know

T0036126

8.   Hospitality

23.   When not to design

38.   How to collaborate

57. What is current and how that creates currency[2]
58. That there is no magic to design
59. How to transcend the limitations of reform
60. That definitions belong to the definers, not the defined[3]

2. Marshall McLuhan
3. Toni Morrison

67. How failure is the only way to success[4]
68. Planning
69. How to assess and iterate
70. How to say no
71. How to present ideas
72. How to defend ideas
73. How to make decisions
74. Not to give excuses
75. To believe in the power that you have[5]
76. Vulnerability
77. To understand emotions
78. The dangers of featuritis
79. To not limit oneself by the imaginations of others[6]
80. How to make time

4. Leonard Bernstein
5. Alice Walker
6. Mae Jemison

81. Edward Said
82. bell hooks
83. Frantz Fanon

*Entries marked with an asterisk are from Sorkin's original list.

*105. What the client wants
*106. What the client thinks it wants
*107. What the client needs
*108. What the client can afford
*109. What the planet can afford
 110. How our designs shape the world
       and this in turns shapes us
 111. The meaning of wicked problems
*112. The theoretical bases for modernity
       and a great deal about its factions and
       inflections
*113. What post-Fordism means for
       the mode of production

*114.   Another language

*121. Accidents must happen
*122. It is possible to begin designing anywhere

*129. How to get lost

*130. The reasons for the split between ~~architecture~~ design and engineering

131. The reasons for the split between design and art

*132. Many ideas about what constitutes utopia

133. Imagined dystopias are some people's realities

*134. Woodshop safety

*135. The architectural impact of colonialism on cities in the [Global South]

*136. A distaste for imperialism

*160. [Some] Geography
161. Sociology
162. Politics
163. History
164. A basic understanding of economics
165. Of engineering
166. Of science
167. Of public health

176. Adobe Creative Suite
177. New technology
178. Open source technology
*179. Club ~~Med~~ Tropicana[7]

7. Wham!

*184. Good model-making techniques in wood, cardboard, [paper, foam and clay]
185. The printing process
186. The effects of noise pollution
187. Of visual pollution
188. How certain emblems and symbols make people feel
189. Different forms of packaging
190. Trends
191. Manufacturing processes
192. Prototyping
193. The difference between prototyping and manufacturing
194. Consumption culture

222. Why the lone designer genius is a myth

*223. How to play a musical instrument
224. Improv
225. How to dance
226. The feeling of the ocean
*227. Which way the wind blows
*228. Where north (or south) is
*229. How to give directions, efficiently and courteously
*230. The diameter of the earth
*231. The number of gallons of water used in a shower

240. To be empathetic.
Truly,
madly,
deeply.

Designerly ways of knowing:
a working inventory of things a designer should know
Danah Abdulla

Onomatopee 214

Author: Danah Abdulla
Publisher: Onomatopee
Graphic Design: Sonia Dominguez & Rob van Leijsen
Printer: KOPA, Lithuania
Printrun: 2000
Typeface: Jane (Monkey Type)

ISBN 978-94-93148-80-2

For Michael Sorkin (1948-2020), and for Palestine.

First edition, 2022

Onomatopee Projects
www.onomatopee.net

Danah Abdulla is a Palestinian-Canadian designer, educator and researcher interested in new narratives and practices in design that push the disciplinary boundaries and definitions of the discipline. She is Programme Director of Graphic Design at Camberwell, Chelsea and Wimbledon Colleges of Arts (University of the Arts London). Danah obtained her Ph.D. in Design from Goldsmiths, University of London and is a founding member of the Decolonising Design platform. From 2010-2016, she ran Kalimat Magazine, an independent, nonprofit publication about Arab thought and culture. Her research focuses on decolonising design, possibilities of design education, design culture(s) with a focus on the Arab region, the politics of design, publishing, and social design.